T0195086

ARE YOU
SERIOUS?

AJ FREEMAN

authorHOUSE®

AuthorHouse™
1663 Liberty Drive
Bloomington, IN 47403
www.authorhouse.com
Phone: 833-262-8899

© 2022 AJ Freeman. All rights reserved.

No part of this book may be reproduced, stored in a retrieval system, or transmitted by any means without the written permission of the author.

Published by AuthorHouse 01/31/2022

ISBN: 978-1-6655-5050-5 (sc)
ISBN: 978-1-6655-5048-2 (hc)
ISBN: 978-1-6655-5049-9 (e)

Library of Congress Control Number: 2022901819

Print information available on the last page.

Any people depicted in stock imagery provided by Getty Images are models, and such images are being used for illustrative purposes only. Certain stock imagery © Getty Images.

Scripture quotations marked KJV are from the Holy Bible, King James Version (Authorized Version). First published in 1611. Quoted from the KJV Classic Reference Bible, Copyright © 1983 by The Zondervan Corporation.

This book is printed on acid-free paper.

Because of the dynamic nature of the Internet, any web addresses or links contained in this book may have changed since publication and may no longer be valid. The views expressed in this work are solely those of the author and do not necessarily reflect the views of the publisher, and the publisher hereby disclaims any responsibility for them.

CONTENTS

ACKNOWLEGEMENTS

First of all above all, I thank God for Jesus. I appreciate the consistent love that The Lord shows me every day. I thank God for The Holy Ghost who keeps me from falling. I want to acknowledge my Dude's, LT, Tyler & Travis. I acknowledge grandparents, the late James and Catherine Tyler. I want to acknowledge my parents David R Freeman Sr. and Katherine Faye Freeman, my brother David R Freeman Jr. and my sister (my heart) Tammy Ellis. I also would like to acknowledge Mother Gloria Bryant and Ms. Andrea Felton for their untiring support. Also, all of my family and friends, The Supt. George L. Carter, and all of those who have and continue to believe in me and my ministry. I acknowledge my mentor, the late great Bishop CL Bryant, and also The Archbishop Q S Caldwell. There are so many others whom I owe gratitude, so if I did not mention you, you know who you are, and you are Loved. Even though there were many who doubted me and did not wish me well, but through my Lord and Savior I was able to accomplish goals that I set for myself, in spite of.

Thank You!

FOREWORD

Bishop Anthony J. Freeman's book "Are You Serious?" chronicles a journey in faith that is inspiring, edifying and insightful to a person of any age. Faith in God is an active reliance on Him, not a passive claim about His steadfastness. Through his intentional reflection on the stories of his childhood upbringing and personal life, Bishop Freeman defines faith as a conviction of what we hope will actively manifest. It is through his accounts of admirable figures in his family and community that we discover faith in God is a choice, not a feeling. As he explains his intricate journey to becoming the Man, Minstrel, and Episcopate that he is today, we see without a doubt numerous instances where we make the decision to trust in the wisdom and logic of God's grand plan—that which we cannot clearly understand— even though we dislike its details.

By faith we agree that God's highest intention incorporates more than the decency of our current circumstances. Bishop Anthony J. Freeman points us to a place where we can acknowledge that it also includes our understanding of His excellence and the effectiveness of our ministry, now and in the future.

I would highly recommend this book to any individual or ministry who finds themselves on the journey to developing an intimate relationship with God combined with initiating a steadfast faith that will aid them in making a series of never-ending decisions to trust God in every space of their lives.

Archbishop Q.S. Caldwell
Chief Apostle and Presiding Bishop of The Celebration of Praise Ministries, Inc.

INTRODUCTION

So let me start off by saying, if "life is like a box of chocolates, you never know what you gonna get." (From the movie "Forrest Gump") Some of mine are melted, because my life has not turned out the way I thought or intended it to be. Life has different challenges and obstacles that change us. This book is about some of the highs and lows of my life. The title "Are You Serious" was chosen because I believe that we sometimes take life too seriously. We don't laugh enough at ourselves because we are too busy laughing at others to take the attention off ourselves. As you read each chapter you will see that my life has not always been easy. I had to endure some things because it comes from within. The upbringing of my Grandparent's faith helped to sustain me while the fantastic four saved my life. I look back at some of the things I did and I have to ask myself, "are you serious right now?"

If you are looking for a book that is full of Spiritual perfection and obtained goals, this is not that book. This is a book of Testimonial Experiences and lessons of Encouragement to lift your spirits and inspire you to confidently move forward. As the "Church Folks" would say, help encourage you to "Run on, and see what the End is gonna be." This is not a book full of sermons and spiritual rhetoric, but it is to serve as a foundation of reflection and help you look back in your own life. You have more victories under your belt than you realize. We, who have given our Heart and lives to The Lord Jesus, can unequivocally admit in an honest way that life has not always been easy.

I have made mistakes I wish that I could go back in time and change, but you know as well as I, we can't do that. I do believe in transparency. I don't see how we can help people that are really hurting, unless we put down our titles and gold crosses. People need to hear someone they can relate to.

It is my prayer that you will be inspired, and encouraged as you laugh and maybe cry a little and see how it possibly relates to your own personal life.

CHAPTER 1

IT'S NOT ALWAYS EASY

It's Not Always Easy

Our Journey on this road of Salvation can sometimes be lonely while subsequently suffering for being misunderstood. Sometimes, it is much easier to cuss someone out than it is to do as 2 Timothy 2:3 (KJV) says, "Endure Hardness as a good soldier." However, if we want to please The Lord, it is going to take endurance. Yes, I know I said cuss someone out. In transparency, I have not done that since I gave my life to Christ. Nevertheless, it sure does not mean that they did not deserve it. There is still a part of me that is not saved. It is called "the flesh." Christ is calling for us to keep it under subjection. In other words, control your tongue and your attitude. I have learned that God does not judge us on how people treat us, but on how we respond to the way they treat us. He is a good God. He is calling for us to endure! That notion, in itself, is not always easy. There are times that you know that you are right. The Holy Ghost will tell you, "Don't say anything. Don't try to defend yourself." Trust me when I tell you, that it takes real faith and endurance. However, it is not always easy.

One of the most frustrating times in my life was, thinking that I heard God and only to find out later, that it was my emotions. Whether it was starting a ministry, or just getting a home, I lived by the notion that if I lived right, and spent time in prayer, that God would speak to me about any situation that I found myself in. But I finally come to realize, that everything that happens is NOT GOD! The situation may simply be a place where God told you not to go, but we sometimes make it God because we don't want to admit that it is our flesh in control at that moment. I also learned, that sometimes my greatest and most powerful enemy is not the devil, it is me, trying to control ME. I want to do what I want to do sometimes so bad, that I will try to equate it with scripture, and make it sound like The Holy Spirit. I wish I had a witness.

We, as preachers and Ministers of The Gospel, must be very careful that we do not promote "this salvation walk as easy." That notion is a lie straight from the pit. If every day that you have *been saved has been ice cream and cake and you have not had any problems, then I have to question. Who you are really following? In 2 Timothy 3:12 we are reminded that, "Yea, and all that will live godly in Christ Jesus shall suffer persecution." There will be difficult days, but do not get it twisted. Just because it is difficult doesn't mean that it is the end. We who live for Christ and have him dwelling inside, recognize that He is the only one who helps us to get through.*

I know that it can be extremely difficult at times, but giving up should never be an option. You should not even have it as an option on the table. You will never reach God's destiny for your life that way. Remember God is Omniscient, which means that He is all knowing. What you are dealing with is not new to Him. He is allowing you to go through for His Glory. No, it's not always easy, but go through. Whatever test you take that you do not pass, you are due to repeat. Some tests are easier than others. You have to ask yourself, "Am I ready to pass this one, or do I need more time in prayer?" Our God is so kind to us that He will never give you a test that you could not pass. If He gave it to you, you can pass it! Successful completion is guaranteed! I believe that one of the biggest problems that we have before and during a test is fear. Some of us are afraid that we will not pass, so we think negatively and talk the same way.

I was blessed with a Great Dad, when I was growing up, who never gave up. He worked for a company that made trucks in Springfield, Ohio. When he was hired, it was a blessing. However, they would lay him off for about 6 months at a time. He would work for 6 months and then he might be laid off for 2 years. They would call him back. He would work for about another four to six months and they would lay him off again. The cycle continued for about ten years, yet he never gave up. He would work tedious jobs until they would call him back. I do not ever remember seeing him at home sitting down and complaining and saying, "These so and so Jokers laid me off again." If I can be honest, it is probably what I would have said. He is what I call Resilient. Resilience is defined as able to withstand or recover quickly from difficult conditions. He stuck with that job until he retired from that job. I wonder how many of us, my age or younger, can say that we would hang in there like that. The older folks did whatever they had to do to take care of their families. They were not perfect, but they were providers. We live in a society that wants everything given to them as easily and quickly as possible.

This is such a microwave generation. If you are going to obtain what you were promised by God, you will have to admit that the process is not easy. Nevertheless, it is profitable.

One of my favorite movies of all time is "Men of Honor" with Cuba Gooding Jr. The movie is about an African American man who decides that he wants to be a Navy Deep Sea Diver. He is not just the only African American to do this, but he is also the first. At the beginning of the movie, he has to pass a test in order to be considered. He fails it, but the teacher encourages him to get a tutor. He goes to the library to find one. He tries to swoon a woman into helping him, but she kept rejecting him. He kept being persistent until finally she asks him, "Why do you want this so much?" He says, "Because they said I couldn't have it!" If you are going to be good at anything you will have to be persistent. If you are going to be great at anything, you must be resilient. Going through is one thing, but getting through the process is something else. In order for you to get to the other side of through, you have to go through while enduring and demonstrating patience in the process. I heard a comedian say, "If Jesus was like us, when they put Him on the whipping post to strike him with the cat o' nine tails, he would have quit after that first strike. Jesus would have said, "Owwwwwww!!!!!! Alright that is enough! I...I...Father, I can't do this. You are going to have to get somebody else. They are not worth all that." My grandmother would say, "Aren't you glad that He stayed there?"

Aren't you glad that He is not like us? He could have very easily called for angels to stop the whole thing immediately, but He saw you. He saw me. He saw that we were going to need a Savior. He knew that it was not going to be easy, but He endured for us. Trusting God is not always as easy as some people claim it to be. You have to grow to trust Him. I do not know why, but for some reason, the struggle we went through, did not seem as bad as we imagined after we finish going through the process. It is the process. It is like getting a prophetic word. When you first hear the word, you are excited about what The Lord has promised you. You think about receiving the promise. That is a wonderful thing, but the problem occurs when you have to go through the process. The Lord does not always tell you how long you have to wait until it is manifested. I wish I had a witness? I said, "I wish I had a Witness?"

As a Minister of The Gospel of Jesus Christ, it is easy to stand behind the podium. We can proclaim that God can provide and He *will see you through to a bunch of people that are really struggling. Anyone worth their weight in ministry can say that sometimes we have to go through it either right before you preach it, or soon after. Nothing beats experience. A story told in Fiction sounds different than a story of non-fiction. People can feel you when you are saying something that they can relate to. They can tell if it is real or not. Your style and demeanor may be second to none, but your heart should be pure to preach this gospel. There are a lot of Biblical orator's that can speak well, but they have a raggedy lifestyle. I am in no way shape or form saying that preachers are perfect. We are not at all. If they tell you that they are, take a couple of steps to the left because something might fall from the sky. God will share His Glory with No one.*

To those of you who did not know, let me tell you. Preachers have to go through the fire as well. It is not always easy. This Gospel carries an anointing that will change the atmosphere. It will change anyone in it. The Anointing is God's ultimate, unrelenting, yoke destroying, burden removing, and atmosphere changing Power. He gives it to those who have a task or a work that they are to do. Please understand, the anointing cost and it is not free. It is not as simple as the laying on of hands. It is getting in the mud, spiritually, and making sure that you come out spotless. Most preachers that you would consider anointed, are the ones that have been through some things that might make you cringe. It took that for them to be anointed by God. Ask yourself, "Am I really anointed, or am I animated and talented?" The answer is found when you go through those tough times. The real you shows up during a fire, and everything in you comes out.

Ephesians 4:11-15 says, "And he gave some, apostles; and some, prophets; and some, evangelists; and some, pastors and teachers; for the perfecting of the saints, for the work of the ministry, for the edifying of the body of Christ: till we all come in the unity of the faith, and of the knowledge of the Son of God, unto a perfect man, unto the measure of the stature of the fullness of Christ: that we henceforth be no more children, tossed to and fro, and carried about with every wind of doctrine, by the sleight of men, and cunning craftiness, whereby they lie in wait to deceive; but speaking the truth in love, may grow up into him in all things, which is the head, even Christ."

Nowhere in these verses does it say that it will be easy. Way too many preachers are being seduced rather than being called. I always say, "If you think that The Lord called you, you need to check the caller ID. Make sure it was Him and not your emotions or people."

Let me say this as well, just because your Grandmother or your best friend said that you should be a preacher, does not mean that you should start a ministry.

The biggest influencer in my life beside my family members was the late great Bishop C.L. Bryant. He was the Pastor when I was a member of The Progressive Church of God In Christ in Denver, Colorado. I would study him and sit on the front pew every service with a memo pad and a pen. I would write down different things that he said. I did that for two years. One day, I had a meeting with him and said "Bishop, I think that The Lord is calling me to preach." If you knew Bishop, you know that not too much rattled him. He just looked at me, while drinking a cup of coffee, and said "OK." I am thinking "Wait, Bishop did you hear me?" He just seemed so nonchalant about it. I could not understand. Did he not care? Should not he be happy that I am following God's instructions? He literally just sat there and looked at me for about twenty seconds and said, "OK." It was not until later that The Lord revealed to me the nature of his response. Bishop knew that this is not going to be easy. The weight of Ministry is not something that you can pick up and put down when it seems too heavy. This is your life! I honored that man. *Any time I was going to make any major decisions in my life, I called him. I knew that he had more than wisdom and he had love to share. I called him one day and told him that this was too difficult for me. I was wondering what I should do. Bishop said, "The preacher is always the preacher, even if they are not preaching. If you are called by God to preach, you will preach even if you decide to live in sin." That blew me away. When you are called by God, the best examples are sometimes caused by the worst experiences.*

It is unfortunate, but there are a whole lot of doctrines in the church. They are changed every day by men and women of their own faith who have pimped out the gospel for hundreds of dollars. When they started out in Ministry, it was about Jesus. At present, it is about the almighty dollar. Too many people are being seduced by money and notoriety instead of the anointing. This is why it is not easy. It is going to take real faith. Real men and women of God who refuse to sell out and get caught up in the prophecy gang, I know what I said; It is a gang. They are trying to recruit more people by switching words and prophe-lying to the weak and vulnerable. There are people being tossed to and fro. They do not know what to believe. We talk about them behind the pulpit as if they are the only problem. In actuality, we must take some of the blame. We complain about what they are doing wrong when they are trying to model what we preach. I am finding that we preach more about their sin and their mistakes rather than the love of Jesus. As a result, they look for a Ministry or a church that is not so judgmental. We say things like, "Well, they just don't want to hear the truth!" In reality, they want to know how to stop what they are doing instead of someone telling them to just stop what they are doing.

These are the last days. People need to know that Christ loves them. It is very easy to preach to them, but it is not always easy to break traditions and legalism. I am thinking the same way an old Louisiana grandma, who only had a 2ⁿᵈ grade education was thinking, when she was trying to save her church from bankruptcy in the early 1900's. All the men were angry and confused at a business meeting, but when mother stood up everybody got quiet. She said "Bredren, It are hard, but it can be did." So just keep in mind, while you are being effective in the things of God, it is not always easy, but it can be done.

CHAPTER 2

IT COMES
FROM WITHIN

It Comes From Within

The greatest quote that I have ever heard in my life came from Bishop Dale Bronner. He said, "When you are born, you look like your parents; when you die, you look like your decisions." It is one of the greatest quotes because it is one of the greatest truths in life. If we are honest, how many decisions have we made within the last three days that have affected our current situation that we are in right now? What brought us to this place? Everything is not the devil. Some things are just life choices that brought us here.

I grew up in Springfield, Ohio. Although it was not a big city like Dayton, Cincinnati, or Cleveland, it still was fun growing up there. I went to The Full Gospel Church of God In Christ where

I learned Spiritual Discipline and some great life lessons. It was old time Holiness. I mean Old time Holiness. Did you hear me? I said, "Old time Holiness!" It seemed as if we were not allowed to do anything! These children today do not know the struggle. We were at church every Sunday morning. Wednesday night was Bible Study. Friday night was the Pastor's night and then back again on Sunday morning. Sunday school started at 11:45 and Morning Service was after that. On a regular Sunday, if we got out of church before 3:00 p.m., it meant that we had another service at 3:30p.m. If the pastor was feeling anointed, we would have evening service at 7:30 p.m. Needless to say, I know Church!

I remember bringing my homework to church with me on the week nights and trying to finish it in the back. There was no way that you would tell your parents "I can't go to church because I have a lot of homework." You might as well say, "I can't stop the pain that is on my backside." I learned a lot from Bishop C.H. and Overseer Mattie M Brantley. That kind of teaching will never leave you. I have to admit that there were some days I wish I could do anything else, but church. When I had the opportunity to not go, I took it. However, if you are a Holiness baby like I was, you also would have to admit that the old-time way will not leave you. You may not practice or do the same traditional things that they did, but it is in you. There is absolute truth to Proverbs 22:6 (KJV) – "Train up a child in the way he should go: And when he is old, he will not depart from it." Even though I tried to not do anything that remotely resembled church, I would find myself singing gospel in the shower. I would witness to someone at the club about Jesus. If it is in you, it is just in you.

God would always put me around people who grew up like I did. A perfect example of that is my sophomore year at Central State University. It was three of my best friends who hung out on the regular. I, Maurice, Lenny, and Kevan were always together. Maurice and I were usually going to parties every weekend. However, one Saturday night, we convinced Kevan to go with us. Kevan was the "saved one" in the bunch. He was so churchy. While we were there, after about twenty-five minutes of prying, we finally get Kevan to come out on the floor with us and the girls we were dancing with. Maurice and I, with a couple other guys, were dancing in sync and showing off our moves. Kevan gets in the middle of all of us and starts shouting on beat with the music. Let me tell you, it was Praise Dance Personified.

Songs like, "Do the Humpty Hump, Do the Humpty Hump" were in full rotation. He did not care what song was playing. He was going to shout. We could not stop laughing because when it is in you, it's just in you!

I think that one of our problems is that we know too much. We are so engrossed with Master's and Doctorate degrees that we seem to forget about the true love of Jesus. I am not calling for us to go back to legalism and tradition. I am saying that we cannot forget what we were taught. This current generation is just living any kind of way and still calling it God. It is our responsibility to teach them. We cannot brow beat them into submission or even make them think that we are better than they are because of our background. We must remind them that Jesus is after a relationship with them. It took me years to understand that. I thought that if you live right Heaven belongs to you. However, you can live right, and still go to hell. It is about a personal and intimate relationship with God the Father through The Lord Jesus Christ. Once you realize that, you will not have to try and impress God with your Gift that He has already given you. You can just be yourself, but remember you cannot serve two masters. As the older saints used to say, "You can't straddle the fence." The problem with straddling the fence is, when you rip your pants, you expose yourself more than you should. I do not know anyone who wants everyone to know all of their business.

I personally have made enough mistakes. Sometimes I wonder, "God, how can you still Love me like you do?" I think that we do more damage than good when we are not at least a little transparent. You cannot help anyone who is going through their issues unless you are honest with them about yours. I am a Bishop in The Lord's church, but I have still failed Him. Just imagine that you are telling others how to trust God no matter what, even while you are going through a divorce. You still keep preaching as if nothing happened when your divorce court date is the next day. It is so easy to tell people how to get through when you have never been in a situation yourself. But it is much easier to tell them that they can make it through it when you did. I literally hate telling my story of my past because it exposes me in a way that would reflect poorly on me. My remaining silence cannot help you.

I remember the days that I would wonder why I am still on this earth. Let me tell you something that maybe you didn't know; depression is a real thing. I think that we can sometimes become so *spiritual, that we forget about human emotions. One of the greatest influences of the enemy is condemnation; it is his job to remind you of all that you did sixteen years ago, and still try to make you feel bad about it. And he will push you so much, that it will cause you to go into, and live in, depression. It doesn't call you before it comes over, it doesn't even knock on your door, depression has a way of slipping in without you knowing it. There are a lot of people who don't know it because they wear it well, it's a mask, and that mask is flawless. It matches everything that you have on, but remember, it's still a mask that hides you from the outside and only shows what you don't cover. That's the one thing about depression, you still have to deal with it, but you don't have to wear it. In 2017, The National Institute of Mental Health lists the prevalence of having a major depressive episode was seven percent, that's a pretty high percentage. It is an emotion that will keep you from God, and you can have it so long that you no longer call it depression, you call it "I'm just tired."*

Do not allow yourself to be caught up in how bad you messed up, because condemnation will try to remind you of all the wrong that you did. But a great exercise to defeat that, is to remember all that you didn't do, and give God the praise for that. I have always enjoyed my life and had never entertained or contemplated suicide, but I did while going through my divorce. There were times I would drive over a bridge. I wondered if, I just speed up and turn the wheel real fast, could I jump this bridge? Who would miss me? I believed that my sons, parents, my brother, sister and a few family members would. For me, at least, I would not have to deal with this tormenting pain.

Let me stop and make a disclaimer here: If you have been married to the same spouse for years and have never been divorced, I want to say congratulations! We salute you! However, do not look down on those whose marriages failed. You have no idea what plagues the thoughts of those who are experiencing these types of torment. There is a tearing away of the heart that comes with divorce. It is a death of a relationship. Let me say this as well, you do not feel anything, if there is a lack of effort put into it. Dealing with death is not easy. And even though there were days of defeat, I remembered that I still have something within me that tells me to fight on to the future, because there is still destiny for me to reach. That is how I made it. I remember at times I would be a guest speaker at a large church event. One of the pastors would have words and say, "I thank God for my first and only lady. We have been married for twenty or thirty years."

While the church would be clapping for him and his precious bride, he would turn around and look right at me. I thank God for The Holy Ghost. Even when you know that you are being scandalized, you should never retaliate. Even though you might want to, and trust me when I tell you, I wanted to, it is not worth it. You should always remember that The Lord is watching our every move and our thoughts. To be honest, you do not have to worry. Jesus said, "What is done in the dark, will be brought to the light." God will give you recompense. Some of those same pastors are unhappy in their own lives that they have the mask on of someone that looks happy. It amazes me the many people that try to be something they are not. They act as if they are better as someone else, rather than themselves. Just be yourself.

There is an old saying, "Be who you is, not who you aint, cause when you aint what you is, you is, what you aint!"

God made only one of you, and you are The Most Beautiful You that He could make, He didn't mess up at all, He perfected the Love of His life, YOU! If you compare yourself to others, you will never realize how beautiful you really are, woman or man. I believe that is what a lot of people (even in the church) are dealing with today, it's a spirit of low self-esteem. Maybe somebody (even in your family) told you when you were a child that you were ugly, and you will never have a pretty woman or a handsome man. As a result of them saying that to you, you feared that when you do find someone, they will leave you for someone else. There are some people who struggle with low self-esteem, but you don't always know it, because they learned how to replace it with confidence. A person really struggling with low self-esteem, will always ask you to tell them if they are handsome, or how pretty they look every time that you see them. And you will know when they have overcome it when they no longer need your affirmation. They can have a piece of broccoli stuck between their teeth, and they will just wipe it off and keep going.

Let me tell you something, it is important to Value You, I am not talking arrogance, but Confidence! When you walk into a room, your confidence should speak before you open your mouth. Confidence in who you are and what God made you to be. Now, it is important to understand that "You don't think yourself more highly than you ought to think, according to scripture, but you need to be confident in who you are. Don't strut around like a proud peacock, but as Bishop C.L. Bryant use to tell me, "walk and smile with a millionaire look, even if you have nothing but lint in your pocket." It is amazing to me the many people who think that you are arrogant and conceited when you are just confident, and most of the time they think that about you, because they are not really sure of themselves. Confidence comes from within, it's not a feeling, it is an assurance, because if it's in you, it's just in you. You will either have confidence or you will have low self-esteem, you cannot have both at the same time, one of them will be in control. For example, if you have low self-esteem, you will complain about how you don't like the way that you look, your nose is too big, or you are too short etc.… But if you are confident, you see your flaws but look in the mirror every day, smile and say, "Thank You Jesus, I am beautifully and wonderfully made!" And you say it with confidence not arrogance. Because there is a distinct difference between the two, a confident person knows who they are, but an arrogant person needs to convince others that they are, what they are not. With confidence you understand, but with arrogance you exaggerate, confidence is self-assure, arrogance is insecure, arrogance has to show off, but confidence will just rest.

I have to admit that I was not the most attractive man in high school or college, and when a pretty young woman showed me any type of interest, I thought immediately that I was all that, until someone better looking came along, and I thought that was why they dropped me. I kept dealing with it until I got tired of that, so I grew to Love Me. Because sometimes you won't change until you get sick and tired of being sick and tired! My Pa Pa used to tell me all the time, "Anthony, beauty is skin deep, but ugly is to the bone!"

Do you really Love You? I can answer that by asking you the question, how do you treat you? Because a lot of us will treat others better than we do ourselves, and that is not right. Jesus did not say "I've come that only certain people might have life, and that more abundantly," and then leave you out. **NO**, that includes you! You have to enjoy you. I make it a point to enjoy my life everyday no matter who likes me or not, because there will always be someone who doesn't like you, but most of the time it is because they don't understand you, or the choices that you made. I try to watch at least a half hour comedy every day, (usually Martin, Frasier, or The Golden Girls etc.....) and laugh with someone every day, usually Supt. G.L. Carter. Because life is too short to not enjoy it. I try to laugh a lot, if you ask me what kind of movie do I want to watch, I will say a comedy every time.

I know we as believers will tell you that Jesus is in love with you, or Jesus thinks that you are Beautiful, but to be honest, even though we know and believe that, we still want somebody to love us down here on earth as well. But if you don't believe that you are capable of being loved for real, you will always find yourself in a relationship with someone that you tolerate, and you tolerate them not because you want to be with them, but because you don't want to be alone. I wish I had a witness. The problem with that is, when you just tolerate someone, you are actually bored with them, and boredom usually creates other outside interests. So before you go down that path, Value YOU first.

I didn't really know what that meant until I dated Robin. Robin was a person that was confident in herself before she met me. She taught me a lot about me, by just being her. We always enjoyed our time together. One night, we are out on a date, and I loved her but I was not confident in myself. As a result I became very jealous, she was pretty, and was built the way I liked………. Oh sorry, I digress, and she was constantly being hit on by other men, but she would always try to reassure me, "Tony, I am with you, and you only," but because of the lack of confidence in myself,

I heard, "Tony, I'm with you until someone better comes along." Because that is what low self-esteem and a lack of confidence in yourself will hear, doubt and unbelief. So every time a guy would walk by, I noticed him looking at her before she did, and I bothered her about it all night. "Did you see that guy.…..." So when dinner was over and we went back to her house, I immediately picked up the remote, because I'm thinking that we are getting ready to watch a movie, she says to me "can you put that down please, I want to talk to you for a minute." "Sure," she sits down and says "Tony, you know that I love you, but before I met you I had peace, and although I want to be with you, I know what Peace is like, and if I have to choose between you and peace, I choose peace, so if you can't cut out this jealousy, I'm going with peace." WAIT, WHAT!? ARE YOU SERIOUS? Let me see if I can get this straight, you choose something that you can't see or even touch over me? Robin made it very clear to me that "Peace can save your life, but the opposite of peace is chaos, and it's a matter of life and death, which all stems from a relationship with God, and NOBODY is worth sacrificing that relationship." That right there, is LIFE!

You have no idea how many people are watching your life and watching the choices that you make. You will not know until you get to Heaven how much you have helped them. You may think that your life is insignificant or uneventful. Trust me, you are helping someone live. You just do not know it yet, and it all comes from within.

CHAPTER 3

MA MA &
PA PA KIND
OF FAITH

Ma Ma & Pa Pa Kind of Faith

If there are any two people that I miss most out of my life, it is definitely my grandparents. I affectionately called them Ma Ma & Pa Pa. These two lived a life of example. All of their children and grandchildren are better for it. My grandfather was about 6', but my grandmother was about 6'1. Pa Pa always called her "Shorty." If you wanted to have a good day, stop by their house in the morning. They had a way of making us laugh with their little love spats. Grandma would say something like, "Jim, I told you three times to come get your breakfast." Pa Pa would respond, "Aw Shorty, I'm coming. I'm coming." Then he would look at me and say, "She is always yelling at me." You have to understand that my Pa Pa was different. He was a "good different." He believed in God and the love for his family. Trust me, when I tell you, he was a man of faith.

My mom, uncles and aunties told me the story of when they were small. He was working at a publishing plant in Springfield, Ohio. While he was working, he heard The Holy Ghost tell him, "Go to New York." He asked The Lord, "Where?" The Lord said, "Go!" He went home and told Ma Ma, "Shorty, get the kids dressed and packed. The Lord said for us to go to New York." Ma Ma said, "What, Jim? It is the middle of the night." Pa Pa said, "I know, but I heard the Lord say Go!" Ma Ma, being the submissive wife that she was, packed all six children and their clothes in the car. They drove to New York. Ma Ma said, "Jim where are we going!" He said, "I don't know." He kept driving. Keep in mind, it was about an eight-hour drive from Ohio to New York. There were no GPS or cell phones to track their distance. All Pa Pa had was faith. They reach Syracuse. My mom said that he was driving and went down the wrong way on a one-way street, and he turned that car around immediately, and pulled up in front of this house. Ma Ma said, "Jim what are you doing?" He said, "I don't know Shorty, but I hear the Lord saying, stop at this house." He gets out, knocks on the door, and there is a woman who comes to the door. She opened it and says, "I've been expecting you." Without knowing who he was, this was amazingly astounding. Keep in mind they have never seen each other a day in their lives. She says, "Do you have your family with you?" Pa Pa says, "Yes." She takes them to a house next door where she had beds and linen already set up and made for all of them. Wow! That act of obedience is called pure faith. I hear so many people talk faith, but I wonder how far they would follow their faith without a cell phone or google maps to guide them. Unfortunately Ma Ma and Pa Pa's faith was not realized, because they returned home a few days later. My Great grandmother and Great grandfather talked them into coming back to Ohio with all of their grandchildren. It's a funny thing about this walk in faith, it's like that old saying that my dad used to tell me, "you can lead a horse to water, but you can't make him drink."

If you are not influenced by a "regardless kind of faith," then your closest friend or family can persuade you from what you know was the will of God for your life. Think about what they missed out on. Whether you know it or not, your acts of faith will help others to walk in faith as well; that actually means that you have to go thru to get thru. Faith is not just a beginning, it is forward movement. And it has to be faith though, because the same people that watch you, are usually the same people that will judge you. Unless you truly trust what God said, their judgements can kill your faith. When you make a true "come to Jesus decision" on something that you know without a shadow of doubt that God told you, you will always have someone say "I don't understand that decision." **NEWSFLASH***…they are not supposed to understand. God didn't give it to them, He gave it to you, and though they may not understand, you will have clarity as you walk it out.*

One of my favorite scriptures is Romans 4:21 that says "and being fully persuaded that, what he had promised, he was able also to perform." You must be fully persuaded to walk in faith. I hear people say that you cannot walk in faith and fear at the same time. I beg to differ with that statement. Sometimes when God tells you to step out in faith, it can be fearful, not a tormenting fear, but a revered caution. But you must still step out in faith. The difference is, your faith has persuaded you, not your fear. For me personally, I have learned that the key element for stepping out in faith, is not asking everybody what they think, because too many opinions will give you too many options. When you hear God, MOVE! Now, it is important to receive wise counsel, but everybody is not wise. Sometimes your enemies are the closest ones to you, and your friends are the ones you don't ask. Walking in faith takes a quiet obedience; it is not loud and boisterous. As the older saints used to say, "You've got to know that you know, that you know."

Mom told me, when she was little, they went on vacation as a family. While they are driving, Pa Pa says, "I think I have a gas leak." Sure enough, there was a gas leak. My Grandpa, being the man of Faith that he was, did not panic. He just drove to the nearest store, went inside and bought all of the children bubblegum. He told them "I need y'all to chew this but don't swallow it." They chewed it until it was gooey. He puts it in his hand, he gets out of the car, gets under the car, and puts the gum on the gas line leak. It took them all the way home without a problem. That is faith! There used to be a song that said, "Faith, Faith, Faith, just a little bit of Faith; Faith, Faith, Faith, just a little bit of Faith. You don't need a whole lot, just use what you got. Faith, Faith, Faith, just a little bit of faith." I have come to realize that God is looking for real faith. This is not the kind of faith that you have to borrow or return. It is the kind that says, "It looks crazy, but I believe God!" This is the kind of Faith that gets God's attention. When you can say, "I don't understand, but I trust you. I don't like this, but I trust you." Show me a man that has no faith. I will show you a man that does not know God! Faith is what God wants.

It is a completely crazy world. They do not understand how you can believe God for a high promotion and have no degree. How you can believe God for a new car when you only make $10,000 a year? It is foolishness to the world according to 1 Corinthians 2:14 that says, "But the natural man receiveth not the things of the Spirit of God: for they are foolishness unto Him: neither can he know them, because they are spiritually discerned."

Faith does not make sense. Faith makes Faith, and dollars make cents. My grandfather had more faith than most people use. There was the story of one year that they had to travel out of town. While they were driving, the headlights go out on the car. As usual, Pa Pa did not panic. He just went to the store, bought some aluminum foil, and put it where the headlights would be. That way, if the police or any other car would be traveling towards them in the opposite direction, the glare of the aluminum foil would reflect back on them and look like they had headlights. That is crazy faith! My grandparents had the "God kind" of faith. There is also the story of them driving home from visiting my family in New York and half way home, they were almost out of gas. Ma Ma said to Pa Pa, "Jim, are we going to make it?" Immediately, Ma Ma began to pray, "Lord, we are your children out here, and we are half way home with no money or gas. Lord, I believe that $5.00 worth of gas will get us home." Gas, at that time, was about 36 cents a gallon. Keep in mind that it is pouring down rain. All of the sudden, she looks outside of the car and sees a green piece of paper. She says to Pa Pa, "Jim that looks like money." Pa Pa said, "Well, then get out of the car and get it Shorty." Now why Pa Pa wouldn't get out of the car for her, and look himself, so she would refrain from getting wet is a question I will have to ask him when I see him in heaven. As soon as he says that, that same piece of green paper blows right to her door. She opens the car door to reach out and get it. Although it is pouring down rain, when she picks it up, it is *a dry $5.00 bill. The bible reminds us that God will supply all our needs according to His riches in Glory. We have to believe for it to happen. Imagine if Ma Ma would have said, "Lord I believe that $50.00 is what we need." It was not the amount of money that was needed, but it is the amount of faith that we must have.*

In our lives, God gives us the option to either have faith or not. He will never force His will upon you. We can choose to complain about our current situation, or we can just believe God. I know that there are some of you who are reading this that can think of when your grandparents, parents or an elder used their faith in a miraculous way. We can either laugh at them, or we can model them. Keep in mind, that when you use your faith, every single decision that you make has a choice. With that, comes revelation. There is a difference between options and choices. Options are the things. Choices are the decision. You can opt out and live in anxiety and fear, or you can choose to believe God. If I were in church right now, I would say, "Look at your neighbor and say, I Believe God!"

One of the reasons why I enjoy the stories of my grandparents' faith is because it proved that life should never be status quo. No two days are the same. Real faith is not stagnant. People that talk faith do not impress me at all because talk is cheap. When you put your faith in action, is when others will take notice. If you are going to use real faith, you cannot be concerned about people's opinions. The truth is that they will have an opinion about you even if you do not use your faith. Some people may ask why is he writing a book? He has divorces under his belt. Those are the same people who are called haters! When you do what people only talk about doing, they begin to hate you because you are doing it before them. They do not hate you, but they hate their own lack of faith. If I am using my faith, I am not worried about what you are doing. I am going to celebrate you. You cannot live your life with the "I hope they like me" attitude. If what is in you brings God Glory, I say, "Hurry up, and Go for it!"

It is imperative that you go to Heaven with a life poured out. In other words, you do everything in this life that you can. The kind of faith that I am talking about does not come from you going to a church service and standing in front of someone and they say, "Receive it!" That is called animation. Real faith, ladies and gentlemen, comes from failing sometimes. However, you still believe God.

In Luke 5:1–11, Peter had spent all night fishing. He was tired, frustrated, and just ready to go home. Jesus gets on his boat and tells him, *"Try again."* He launches out into the deep. Not only is he tired, but his crew and the crew of the other ships that were with him were tired too. They are calling it a night, just washed their nets, and put everything up till later. Jesus says, *"Try again."* Peter could have come up with all kinds of excuses like, *"Lord, are you serious right now? I'm really tired. I know fishing, you know carpentry, stick with what you know, and I will stick with what I know."* But Peter then said *"nevertheless, at thy word, I will let down the net."* In other words, *"I will do it because you say so."* Notice, Peter did not use his excuses, he used his *"Nevertheless,"* which simply means despite what has just been said or referred to. It is a transition into something new; it's turning a negative into a positive. One of the greatest lessons to be learned here, is that you cannot reflect on your failures in the past to determine your future outcome. My closest friend Supt. GL Carter says it this way, *"The only way that you trip on what's behind you, is if you are going backwards."* A *"Nevertheless"* moves you out of the way, so that God can have His Way. It is not mere words but it is implied Faith.

Pa Pa was a good man, but he did make some mistakes, like not filling up his car with gas until it was almost empty. Pa Pa was also a pilot that had a couple of airplanes as well, so there was a time that he did run out of gas in the air and ended up crash landing in someone's corn field. So one day Ma Ma asked my mother "Faye, why don't you ever get in the plane with your father, all of the other children have been in the air?" My mom responded, "Mama, if he runs out of gas down here, I can only imagine what he will do up there." One day my mom was reminiscing and said, "picture it" "we as a family are riding down the road as if nothing is wrong, and then all of the sudden you hear," "I need you kids to help push," "because Daddy ran out of gas in the middle of the road, and made all six of us kids push the car to the gas station."

You will notice that just about every biblical character in the bible had a fall, Abraham, Noah, Moses, David, Peter, etc, but we read about them not just because of their failures, but because they got up from them. I read a phenomenal quote once that read, "There is no real evil in falling, unless you stay there." When I read a book,

I am not impressed by the great words that can be put in a sentence, I am not only intrigued on how you got in a situation, but I want to know, how you got out. Whether you know it or not, your failures have helped you. Ask yourself, are you more analytical, or are you more faith conscious? Because real faith does not try and figure things out before you step out. I think the reason why we try to figure it out is because we have failed in that place before, and fearful that we might do it again. Real faith is hearing Jesus say "Step out" and you do just that. Can you imagine in Matthew 14:25–33 the thoughts in Peter's head being the only one to step out of the boat onto the water. Then, when he begins to sink, Jesus grabs him by the hand and saves him and they both step back into the boat, and then there was peace. Notice, there was no peace until Jesus came back with him. Could it be, that one of the reasons we haven't experienced real faith is because we are too scared that it just might NOT be Jesus? So we don't step out until we have analyzed and strategically understood if it is Him or not? Just a notion, before you condemn Peter, ask yourself, what would you have done? Would you have looked thru the fog and thought "is that Jesus, or a hologram?"

You may have to start with "shopping cart faith" before you can grow to gum on the gas line faith. Just believe that when you go to one of the stores that you need a quarter to get a shopping cart, that there will be a cart waiting for you in the store without the use of a quarter. It may sound simple, but it's a place to start. Because our faith has to grow, you only start off with mustard seed faith. There are some of you who are reading this, the devil tried to kill you a long time ago, but you learned how to recycle fear into faith, and what was meant to kill you, made you live, what was meant to drown you, made you swim, and what was meant to weaken you, made you stronger. And by faith, you will have more victories under your belt.

CHAPTER 4

THE FANTASTIC FOUR

The Fantastic Four

That is why I am eternally grateful for the Fantastic four in My Life. My Jesus, and my 3 sons, LT, (Anthony Jr.) Tyler, and Travis. I can absolutely guarantee you that I would not have made it without them. I remember coming home (when I was married to my 1ˢᵗ wife) after a long work day, and they would rush the door to hug and kiss me when I came in, every single night. I'm tearing up just telling you about it, because those are the memories that saved my life. I remember after the divorce going to their house to visit them after work, and just taking a walk around the block while holding their hands, and LT, who was about five, looked up at me, and said, "Dad, you are my Bestest friend I ever had"…I still have that smile on my face. Priceless.

The song "Falling in Love with Jesus, was the best thing I've ever done," is sincerely my testimony. As I said earlier, it took me years to understand that He Loves Me in spite of me. After I received Him into my life, I would mess up and then try to make myself feel bad (as if that would make God really know how sorry I was). So, I would punish myself by not watching a game or one of my favorite tv shows, and listen to nothing but ole time gospel for two weeks straight. I was so pitiful. I thought that's what God wanted. I came to realize that first of all, it is NEVER ok to sin. 1 John 2:1 "My little children, these things write I unto you, that ye sin not. And if any man sin, we have an advocate with the Father, Jesus Christ the righteous." But, it is also NOT ok for you to try and tell God how He should feel about you either. Once you have asked Him to forgive you, all is forgiven and all is forgotten. We are the ones who put on our scuba gear of regret, and diving mask of our past, and go swimming in the sea of forgetfulness, that's our fault.

It was Jesus that kept me from killing myself; it is Jesus that keeps me even now. I am amazed by people who say things like "God loved me, even when I didn't deserve it." Question, when did you ever deserve it? We don't know how many times we have drunk poison and didn't know it, we don't know how many times someone was plotting our downfall, but God blocked it, we don't know how many times we stopped at a red light and someone tried to pull the trigger on us but their gun jammed, we don't know how many times we woke up in the middle of the night and coughed up cancer or tumors, we don't know. But we do know that He is our keeper and He is worthy of ALL Praise and All Glory! We do know that if it had not been for The Lord on our side....

I remember getting up early one morning to pray, and while I was going through the ritual of the same prayer, I was tired, but I wanted God to know that I was going to be faithful in Prayer, and after about twenty-three minutes of clapping my hands while saying "Thank You Jesus," The Holy Ghost said to me, "what are you doing?" I'm like, "Lord I am praying to you," It was as if the whole house got quiet and then He said, "You know, sometimes, I want to talk first!" So, needless to say, my whole prayer life changed after that day.

God is not into rituals and tradition, if you have a relationship with Him, He is about YOU. Once you grow in your relationship with Him, it is not as easy to sin, don't get it twisted, you still will, *but you will feel so convicted, that even if you called somebody an "ole nasty heifer" behind their back, you will have to repent.*

I can't live without my relationship with Jesus, and to be honest, I don't even want to. That being said, I am so grateful for the Grace and Mercy of God. I do not deserve the sons that I have, when I tell you that I was that bad child, the one that you see as a preacher now, but also the same one whose father said "If you do one more thing wrong, I am going to take you down to the detention home myself." Now please understand, I got my share of whooping's, (I probably got some of yours too). My parents had a long paddle that hung on the closet door that said "Board of Education" and I think my left hind part is imprinted on it. My mom and dad believed in "spare the rod, spoil the child," but I was in trouble EVERY SINGLE DAY. I know that you probably think that I am exaggerating, but it is the truth. I remember back in 1983, my mother said to me "I want to congratulate you, you have been good all this week"....what did she say that for? Because I think that was the last week of a whole week of good behavior. I can't explain it, it was as if I woke up every morning saying (in my English voice) "Please......Mother, Father, May I now have another whooping to start the day?"

So when I tell you that The Lord is KIND to me, it is not an overstatement. My sons have not given me any trouble. I am so blessed, but if you ask my mother, she will tell you that I am the reason that she sings to herself, and yells at her plants, it's because she is having flashbacks.

I remember one summer I had to attend summer school, and instead of just getting through the four weeks of just paying attention and getting out of there, I had to act up. I always wanted to be the center of attention, but the dudes I hung out with, didn't, so guess who always got in trouble?

It was the week of 4th of July, and some of my friends brought firecrackers to school, and for some DUMB, IDIOTIC, STUPID reason, we were lighting them in the bathroom, and the teachers heard it and rushed into the bathroom and guess who got caught, yep you guessed it, the dude who wanted to be the center of attention. The teacher asked "who is lighting the firecrackers?" And while my so-called friends got rid of their evidence, they pointed at me with the exploded firecracker in my hand, and for some odd reason, I felt that lying was the best option. I don't know why we believe that lying will be the best option, because you normally have to tell a lie to tell a lie. I believe that is one of the reasons why God won't let a liar stand before Him in Judgement, because He knows that they are going to try and lie.

I heard the story of a little boy who was in Sunday school and the teacher asked the question, "Does anybody know what a lie is?" And one little boy raised his hand and said "It is when you don't tell the truth", and the teacher said "that's right," but little Byron immediately raised his hand, and began to yell out "Ooooh, Ooooh, I Know, I know," and the teacher said "Yes Byron, what do you think that a lie is?" and Little Byron said, "It is also a very present help in the time of trouble."

So with a spirit of deception and chicanery, I said, "Well Tommy had the lighter and somebody pushed me into him (5 times) and it lit the firecracker." So they sent me home and said "we are going to call your parents", so needless to say, it was a long walk home. Well, I didn't say anything to my parents about it and we went to my grandmothers for a family gathering. While we are there, I'm thinking "cool, my teachers forgot," but really, I am the one who forgot, **that my parents gave the school my grandmother's phone number in case of emergency.** Now why they thought this was an emergency is beyond me; so they called and asked for my Mom, and suddenly my digestive system began to act up, and I can see her face even right now, she went from "I'm very happy to be here," to "I'm going to kill him" in 4.73 seconds. So instead of just confessing the truth, I tried to lie to my parents which was THE ABSOLUTE DUMBEST thing I could have done. My mother said "Boy, do you really think that we are that stupid?" So while my brother and sister ride home with mom in her car, I am riding home in my dad's truck, and he just stopped the truck and looked over at me and said "Boy, be honest, are you on drugs?" No Sir, "well you act like it." There was nothing left to say.

I would not have made it without my sons, sometimes it was not necessarily the conversations that we had, although I really enjoyed them, sometimes it was just their presence that let me know that God wasn't mad at me anymore. It is amazing how life is, when your children are small you think I can't wait until they move out of my house (but in my case, I can't wait until I am done paying child support) but when they graduate high school and college, you seem to worry about them more. My oldest Anthony (LT), was and is in love with basketball since the day of his birth, and he is actually *pretty good; I don't know if he is better than me, but he is pretty good. Let me stop playing, I would have 3 cramps by the time he scored 10 points probably. He is an awesome basketball player, and son, but an even better big brother. He is constantly looking out for someone else's need. My middle son Tyler, was born with a preacher's mic in his hand. His mother and I knew from the day he made noise that God was calling him to ministry. He would grab anything that resembled a microphone (a pencil, pen, straw, etc....) and he was preaching before he could form a sentence, so when he graduated from Ohio Christian University we knew, and know, that Greatness is his portion. My Baby boy Travis, is "That Dude." It is impossible for you to be in his presence for more than five minutes without laughing at something he said or done. God has given him a charisma that is second to none. I remember when he was younger, I went to visit them, and they had just gotten a new television, and they were going to connect an antenna to it. It was brand new in the box, so Travis opens it and begins to hook it up. I said, "Hold on Travis, let's look at the directions first," He looks at me and says, "Dad, it says, this is an antenna, connect it to your TV."*

It really doesn't matter how bad it is in our lives, God always sends someone to help you get through, and for me, it was The Fantastic Four.

I remember when they were small, watching and listening to mommy and daddy argue before the separation and divorce, I couldn't help but wonder that even at that age, what was going thru their minds. I remember one day in particular, my ex and I were arguing and the boys were downstairs, I was so selfish, dogmatic and controlling, I was willing to get my point across, no matter what it took. So she was on the bottom 3 steps, and I was trying to get upstairs and she would not get out of my way, and although I would never hit her, I grabbed her by the ankles and pulled her down the stairs, while all the time arguing and raising my voice. I just happened to look to my left, and there was the most frightening sight, my boys sitting on the couch, all 3 (ages 6, 5, and 3) sitting back as if they were in trouble, looking at their dad, the same dad that they hug and kiss every night, the same dad that they run to the door to meet every day, treat their mother as if she was a sack of potatoes. I remember all three of them had the same "Dad, what are you doing?" look on their faces. They didn't know whether to be mad, or cry or be scared, all

I know is, that the look that they gave me was the look of disgust to God. Ladies and Gentlemen, you really don't know how much you are hurting and damaging your children arguing and fighting in front of them, children remember, even if you forget. And when you choose to argue and fight in front of them, it inevitably leaves a stain. Stains are not always easy to remove, but they are easy to notice. While I am going on with my life as if nothing happened, there is possibly still a stain in their minds, that notices "no matter what my Dad does in his life, and no matter what he accomplishes, I remember that night that we watched him drag my mom down those three stairs by her ankles," and although my ex-wife might have forgiven me, and they might have forgiven me, I still have the stain. I believe that God can remove all our guilty stains, that is Very True, but I also believe that though I know He can, sometimes He won't. It's a reminder, so that when you think that you have arrived, or (as my Aunt Ruth would say) think that you are so suchy much, remember that you are still human, with frailties and mistakes. That is why one of my favorite scriptures in the Bible is Psalm 103:14 "for He knoweth our frame; He remembereth that we are dust." I love the New Living Translation version that says: "For he knows how weak we are; he remembers we are only dust." I am so grateful to Him for His unfailing Love that supersedes my mistakes and sins. I will admit that I was not able to give them all that they wanted when they grew up, but they gave me more than I thought I wanted, they gave me Life! When I asked them what they remember about their parents' divorce, LT and Travis said "not much because you were always around," but Tyler said "not much Dad, but I do remember that day you pulled mom down the stairs." (The Stain)

When I sit in my house and just look at their pictures, I am always amazed at how time went by so quickly. I remember when they were small and my Dad came over for a visit, he saw them running, looked at me and said, "Cherish this time that you have with them, because one day you will look and it will be gone just like that." I looked at him and said "Yes Sir," not really believing that time would go by so fast, and yet here we are in 2021 and I now have a 21 year old, 24 year old, and a 25 year old. Where did the time go? I always thought that I was going to be close with them, until one day I went through the normal routine and took them to school, and did as I always did and kissed them goodbye (which I still do today) and Tyler, who was in the 4th grade at the time, literally pushed me back with his arm and said "Dad, please, not in front of everybody." It was at that very moment, I knew that things were changing.

When they would come to visit with me on the weekends, we would always watch cartoons and just eat, and they had no idea how much they were helping me. I would call them during the week and made sure that even if we talked for just 2 minutes a piece, we would NEVER end a conversation without prayer. There are a lot of things that I can live without, but Prayer is not one of them. Prayer is conversing with God: it is the intercourse of the soul, it is not meditation, but a beseeching and pouring out your deepest concerns and issues before a God who will not judge you. The most Valuable and Powerful resource that a believer has is a prayer life. Your prayer life should always be the weapon of choice, we win more battles in prayer than any other way. I heard them talking one day about three years ago, and they said to each other, "remember when we used to stay with Dad on the weekends and we had to turn up the tv to hear it because Dad would be praying?" To me that was one of the greatest compliments that they could have given me. When I transition off of this earth, I want it to be known that Freeman made some mistakes in his life, he fell a few times, and he even got on our nerves some, but He was a man that truly loved Jesus, and he was a Man of Prayer!

CHAPTER 5

ARE YOU
SERIOUS
RIGHT NOW?

Are You Serious Right Now?

There are some things in my life that I wish that I could reverse or take back, and one of the biggest things is the way that I treated my parents. I said in the earlier chapters that I was always in trouble, but my mom and dad NEVER gave up on me. I have even had some of my cousins tell me that they thought that my dad was going to kill me a couple of times. They were always giving me chance after chance after chance. My mom was that real disciplinarian that would get me, but she would scare me more when she said "wait until I tell your father." Now I am going to warn you that this is the part that I continue to cry about, so while you are reading this, please know that my heart breaks telling it, ok......... and here we go.

As I said before, I always wanted to be the center of attention, so I remember one summer I had done something that my mother said "wait until I tell your father," it was as if she said, "He is going to kill you tonight." I remember I waited until she went upstairs and I took off, I ran away to a friend's house, and when his parents said that I couldn't stay there, I just went walking until it was dark on the north side of town, and I ended up at Mercy Hospital. I went to the emergency room for a while and then to different waiting rooms for a while until a security guard asked me who I was, I took off again. I ended up going back home and spent the night in my dad's tool shed. So in the morning my brother came out to the shed to get something for my dad and he saw me and hugged me and drug me inside the house to my parents. They were so happy to see me that they hugged and kissed on me, and started calling others to tell them that they have found me. My Dad pulled me to the side later that day and said "I should whoop you for this, but I am just glad that you are home," and so I went to bed without punishment.

Now you would think that I would have taken that kindness and done better, but I, and my selfish self, used that against them. What I mean by that is, every time I knew that I was in big trouble, I would run away again. Until one day I will never forget, my Dad was dealing with some health issues, he had just suffered a heart attack, and was coughing a lot. I ran away again for something, and I remember my dad came after me. I was always a pretty good athlete and could run pretty fast, so I would see him, and duck behind buildings or houses, until this time I wasn't looking, and he saw me before I saw him, right at the bottom of the hill by the railroad tracks on Wittenberg St. (If you are from Springfield, OH. you know exactly where I am talking about.) He was crying, and coughing at the same time, he said "Son, get in the car," I didn't want to, but I did. He didn't say anything to me all the way home, when we get to the house, we get out of the car, and he is moving a lot slower than usual, but I didn't really care about that, all I cared about was not getting a whooping. We get to the front door, my mom is standing there, I walk in first, and then he very slowly walks in behind me, while I am walking upstairs to prepare myself for another punishment, my dad takes 3 steps into the living room and then BOOM, he collapses to the floor while still coughing and hurting. My Mother of course is frantic, "Dave, Dave, what's wrong, do you want me to call the ambulance?" I turned around to see him shake his head no, and walked towards him, and my Mom, looks at me right then with disgust in her eyes, and says, "If he dies, it's your fault!"

Now before you condemn her for what she said, understand she was actually right, it would have been my fault, but God was Merciful, and he regained his strength each day. I blamed my mother (silently) for years for that comment, until I had to deal with myself, and let me tell you, there is no uglier person than you, when you really get down to the real you. If you do not take accountability for your actions, you will never be what God intended for you to be. And I literally had to say to myself, "Are you serious right now?" "Are you that self-absorbed that you would rather blame someone else for your wrong?" And the answer was an unfortunate YES!

Listen, if you are going to be truly effective in Ministry, you have to deal with you, before you can deal with other people, because if you don't, you will spill blood on your hands as well as theirs. What is important to grasp here, is that although God will convict you of your wrong, He will never condemn you. The word conviction means to convince a person of their error; but the word condemnation means to pass judgement against someone, the difference is that conviction doesn't judge, but condemnation is a constant reminder of your wrong action. In other words, conviction is what God says, but condemnation is you acting as God, to judge someone.

It is amazing to me, that when you tell people your story or testimony on what God has done in your life, or what He has brought you through, and they immediately say something like, "Wow, that was stupid." You have to get away from that spirit of condemnation, because it will try its best to make you depressed and eventually suicidal. My mother used to say to us growing up, "Be careful what you do and how you treat others, because there are some people that don't go to church or pick up their bible, but YOU will be the only Bible that they will read."

My mom is that person that Loves, but will tell it like it is, she does not sugar coat anything, she said to me while we are riding along in my car one day, and she sees two young women who have on booty shorts, and tank tops, this is our conversation....

"I HATE how some of these young girls are dressing, they are NOT smart and full of the devil,"

"Mom, you can't say that,"

"Oh Yes I can, it's in the bible"

"Where?"

"You know in Luke 8, where Jesus cast out the legion of demons out of the man?"

"Yes Ma'am"

"You will notice that after Jesus cast out the devils, the next time they saw that same man, he was CLOTHED and in his right mind……..he put some clothes on."

Crickets…then uncontrollable laughter…

You know, the older she gets the funnier she gets, but she still tells the truth, whether we want to hear it or not. I think that when God made woman, He put in her a non-filter mechanism that releases at age 65, because most friends tell me that their mother also has no filter. They will tell you how they feel about you or someone else without caring if it hurt your feelings or not.

It is important for you to stay in your lane, if you are going to win this race called life, you have to run where you are appointed only. I used to watch my Mom and Dad, on how they would carry themselves. My mom was the very domestic housewife, unless she had to go out for a season to pick up an extra part time job to help with bills for a minute, but mainly she was at home and made sure that breakfast and dinner was ready every day for her husband and her children. (Where are those kind of women anymore?) I digress, she went out of town one week and Dad was in charge, now Dad did a wonderful job with us, he played with us that week, made sure that we ate, took our baths, and even played games with us, but he kind of stepped out of his lane a little bit. He saw a pile of dirty clothes by the washer and dryer, so he decides to wash them, and he did what he was supposed to, whites with whites and colors with colors, sounds good, UNTIL…he washed mine and my brother Dave's underwear with the old curtains that had fiberglass in them. To be honest, we didn't know until we were on our way to Pittsburgh for a church service on that Sunday, and I started itching and scratching, my brother started itching and scratching, until our skin started to turn red. My Mom comes to the back of the bus where we were and said "what's wrong with y'all, why are you scratching so much?" We told her we didn't know, then her and Dad were talking and she said "Oh my God, Dave you washed their clothes in with those fiberglass curtains!" We laughed it off, but I could tell that my Dad felt bad, he kept apologizing to us. Well, they let us take them off, thank God. That's when I started to really understand the revelation to Stay in Your Lane!

I Love my Mom and Dad with all of my heart, and I had no idea what it took to be an example until I had my own children. My dad was that Dude that tried to do whatever he could to make things work for his family. I remember during his years of being laid off at the factory, he would use a factory credit to get us some new shoes, so he brought home a magazine and asked my brother and I, what kind of shoes we wanted, (I guess there were no girl shoes, so my sister didn't get any) my brother chose boots, and I chose tennis shoes. The simple thing to deduce here, is that, if you are getting shoes from a factory, they are going to be steel toed shoes, no matter what kind of shoe, it will be steel toed. I was so proud of those shoes when he brought them home, that I wore them till the wheels fell off (literally….. you'll understand in a minute). So I noticed one day that they were getting a little looser as I was walking to school than they were normally, but I thought, "Nahhhh, they are probably just still breaking in."

So it was a beautiful day and we went outside for gym class to play kickball, and it was my turn. I considered myself pretty good, so when I was up to kick everyone stood back, including the outfield because they thought that Freeman was going to kick it out of the park. When the pitcher rolled the ball to me, I kicked it as far as I could, and as I was running to first base I noticed that my shoe was flapping and a girl was screaming, all I remember is, that there were 2 flying objects in the air at the same time, one was the ball I kicked, and the other was the steel that came out of my shoe. I just saw kids ducking and trying to get out of the way of a steel attack. But do you think I stopped running? Maaaaaaan listen, I ran the full bases till I reached home to find everyone laughing and pointing at me and my flapping shoe, and to this day, there are some that have not forgotten the boy with the steel toed tennis shoes.

Is it just me, or does anybody else look back at your life, see the mistakes you made, and just want to go back in time, grab yourself by the collar, and say, "Are you serious right now, Don't Do That!!!" I remember growing up my mother would anoint our heads with oil before we went to school. (We who have accepted The Lord Jesus into our heart, believe, that the oil represents the presence of The Holy

Spirit.) I think that helped her more than it helped me, because I would come home from school, and it was like she could see right thru me, and as soon as I came thru the door, she would look at me and say, "Alright, what happened?" And although she was right, I didn't want to tell her, but somehow The Holy Ghost would tell her before I did, or, she had a secret spy at the school, because she always knew when I did something stupid, again.

I remember one summer I had to go to summer school (again), and my uncle Timmy was watching me because my mom, dad, brother and sister went on vacation without me (they did warn me months before, that if I had to go to summer school again, they were going on vacation anyway). So before they left, my mom anointed me with the anointing oil. I was cool, because Uncle Timmy has always been the favorite uncle of the family. And when he went to his house for a while, I grabbed at the opportunity. I took the spare keys of the car outside and drove it around the city (no license and no permission) as if I just bought it off the lot. There I was, seat all the way back, leaning, with just one hand on the wheel, I thought that I was so smooth, UNTIL, I was driving down one of the busiest streets in Springfield and saw Bro. Mike, who went to my church, and oh yeah, he was also a police officer. Now why I honked and waved at him, I don't know, and I didn't realize how much trouble I was in until my parents got home a couple days later. They pulled up, unpacked the car, and my mom walked in, looked right at me, I didn't even say anything yet, but I found out that the oil penetrates thru lies and deceit, and she said "OH Lord, Tony, what did you do? I tried to lie, and said "Nothing," it couldn't have been two minutes later that the phone rang, my mother answered it, and I remembered hearing "Hello.......Oh, yes, I'm fine.....Yes it was a nice trip............. WHAT?!!!!"

I didn't know why, but we had some tattle tale saints in the church, I mean, at least let them rest for a couple of hours, Geeez! So needless to say, I was in trouble again.

My Dad is my hero. He is that man that went to work every day regardless of how he felt, the same man that made sure that his family did not go to bed hungry, the same man that when you look at him at first you will think that he is just mad about something, but he has the biggest heart. It is impossible not to love him. When I was consecrated to The Bishopric in 2017, it seemed as if everybody had an excuse or a reason why they could not make it to Albany GA.

But my dad who was 75 years old at the time, bought himself a plane ticket, and made it out. It was an honor having him there. During the ceremony, they were vesting each of us, and when it came down to putting on the episcopal ring, normally the spouse will put it on the right ring finger which signifies they're authority in the church. I was standing still while I was being clothed by the armor bearer's and only saw out of the corner of my eye, my Arch Bishop QS Caldwell signal for someone to come up front, little did I know that it was my dad. He didn't even know what Bishop was calling him for, and when he got to the front he gave my dad the ring and asked him to put it on my hand. Maaaaaaaann Listen, after he placed it on my finger he gave me the biggest hug and started crying, and of course I did too. It was The Perfect moment for me. I will always honor and appreciate my Arch Bishop for calling him up. While we were riding back to the hotel, my dad just started crying (if you know David Russell, you know he doesn't hardly cry) and with a very soft voice, he said "Wow, I never in a million years thought that I would be able to do that for my son." Then I started crying.

Ladies and Gentlemen, I am not telling you all of these testimonial experiences and giving you these words of encouragement for nothing.

You must understand that I am who I am because of The Grace and Mercy of God. Grace is God giving us what we do NOT deserve, but Mercy is God NOT giving us what we DO deserve.

There will always be people who will criticize you, you will always have bad memories of the mistakes that you made, but, let those be memories that propel you, not reminders that condemn you. You are more than a conqueror! I don't care what anybody has told you, you are Victorious!

I am grateful to The Lord that he does not reward us after our sins, in other words, He doesn't give us the same amount of wrong that we did to Him. Because as you have read in each chapter, I should not even be alive, I should not be able to write a book, and I definitely should not have these 3 men that He blessed me with. If God rewarded me after my sins, I should have 3 roaches as pets in a tiny plastic box that I can't open to take care of, that are already on their back, DEAD!

If you be honest with yourself, are you at least trying to do what you were called on this earth to do? Have you even considered how valuable you are to this earth? We need you! I know you may feel depleted, but you are the person that someone is waiting for. You are being watched, I am not saying that to scare you, but to encourage you that someone likes the way that you make decisions. You are absolutely Beautiful, absolutely Handsome, but it is not your looks that they are watching, and you have something on the inside that is attracting them to you. They may never tell you, and you may never know until you get to heaven who they are, but you have helped someone to live.

Stay the course and keep the faith! If you got out of line, get back in line! If you fell, get up! There is no more time to waste. Laugh, Love, and enjoy your life the way that The Lord wants you too.

COMMENDATION

"Faith is unseen but felt, faith is strength when we feel we have none, faith is hope when all seems lost." –
Catherine Pulsifer

Life is filled with some unexpected challenges, obstacles, and adversities. Each day, we arise with renewed possibility and hope in a God who consistently proves out our purpose by willing us to exist. As stewards of time, we must learn to match God's intentionality and effort through having faith.

Bishop Anthony J. Freeman's book "Are You Serious?" brings to the forefront that everyday life is so much better when you believe. Does it become easier things are ideal, conformable and convenient? No. Faith is a necessary attribute, in the life of the believer because it pushes us to persist in the face of hardship while reaching with zeal towards your end goal.

This book is definitely one that will make you laugh, think, and reflect on some instances in your own life where radical faith was required. Bishop A.J. Freeman inspires us to take another look at what faith is. Faith is the voice inside of you telling you that there are brighter days ahead. Faith is the relentless belief and confidence in God's ability. To have faith is to have eternal consolation in life because whatever happens, there will always be hope.

Dr. Robert O'Keefe Hussell

Pastor and Establishmentarian

The Summit Church Nashville (Nashville, Tennessee)

"Are You Serious?" by Anthony J. Freeman is a book for EVERYONE. A clear down to earth presentation of looking at God, life, and love. Once you start reading this book, it will be hard to put it down. I was forced to pause several times due to laughing until I cried. The author's humor sneaks around and hits you like an unexpected punchline enabling you to understand the serious topics easily. I smiled and laughed while reading this fantastic book. Even after reading, parts will still pop in your head and make you smile."

Lasondra Burks

Author, Entrepreneur, & Motivational Speaker

"Are You Serious" is a transparent account of some of life's lows and highs. It depicts a very vivid story line that spans over several decades. The story is very relatable. The story is very transferable. The story is very real.

We all at some point have struggled with our own spiritual identity. We have had to have a "Come to Jesus" moment. It was then we realized our self worth. And more importantly, we realized our mission in life. "Are You Serious" will help you reflect and think about your own life's assignment.

Moreover, relationships are the foundation of our existence. This book highlights love from many angles. It illustrates agape, storge', and eros love. Love covers a multitude of faults. And at the end of the day it is ALL we need. Are You Serious!

Dr. Angela E. Addison

Bishop Freeman, I truly enjoyed your book entitled "Are You Serious".
It was refilling and refreshing. Your transparency is to be applauded.
Your humor is to be appreciated. You have blessed me beyond words.
I pray God continue to bless you.

Bishop Bertha Hodge

Printed in the United States
by Baker & Taylor Publisher Services